UNPAUSED
POEMS

UNPAUSED
POEMS

real, raw, relevant

Alice Scott-Ferguson

CLADACH
Publishing

UNPAUSED POEMS : Real, Raw, Relevant
©2021 Alice Scott-Ferguson
All rights reserved.

Published by:
CLADACH Publishing
Greeley, CO 80633
https://cladach.com

Cover and Interior Art: Elaine Pedersen
ISBN: 9781945099212

With endless gratitude for a man with a library
of ten thousand books!
For his love of literature, my poetry, and me.
I love you, my Ron.

CONTENTS

INTRODUCTION

Unpaused is my second book of poetry. In contrast to *Pausing in the Passing Places* (my first collection of verse), *Unpaused* invites the reader to ease out of the safety zones and trust the open spaces. This volume of poems extends an invitation to find fresh insights in entrenched views and to share in the wonder of epiphanies encountered in both the sacred and the secular.

During the course of writing this book, there was an exceptionally succulent, yet sobering supply of material for a poet's reflection and her proclivity to ponder and pronounce. An ongoing pandemic threatening to unmoor society as we have known it, and an all time low in race relations in the United States driving deeper divides among us. We have navigated a national election through a hostile highway of acrimony, angst, and anger. Included in this volume are offerings of insight into, and reflections on, facets of such fractious issues.

The title *Unpaused* may be an apt moniker for such a time as this! I am deeply grateful that you hold this book in your hands. May it help you to journey on in hope, without fear, and in increasing awareness of great, all-encompassing Love that guides the uncharted route of our lives, now and always.

I. HURTING and HOPING

THE LIGHT OF LAUGHTER

Until my stomach cramps and I shout "Stop!"
    tears trace my face as my whole being relents to mirth
    and its magic. A funny story, a movie, a comedian
    or my own foolishness and shared humor with a friend
Babies laugh contagious cackles before they can talk
    universal language of our existential loneliness
    rubric of relief from hard knots in our gut
    adhesions of angst enmeshing the mind
Healthy hormones surge, toxic ones take flight
    heart beats with a bigger blood supply
    aches and pains subside
    wellbeing saturates every cell
A distinctly salutary shower for the soul

GRATITUDE'S CHILD

Gratitude gurgles up from the depth
of a satisfied soul

just basking in blessing of being
aware of the source; the stability
of knowing a Father who art in heaven
Who gives daily everything I need
Who can be trusted

Though my soul is severely troubled
thanksgiving wells and swells
tapping the spring of water from inside
that never dries
no matter how parched the ground

Anchored in the eternal ground of being
in the goodness of love
all is more than well
Faith and hope hook hearts
and love is birthed

THE MISSING—

of him
The time
        to pick up from school
        comes and goes now
My car remains parked
        though my heart
        retains the route
The missing becomes the longing
        the wistful looking back
        time cuts no slack
        memories morph into shadows
        standing by the gate of my mind
I let a smile replace the sigh
        as a young man pulls out of the shadow
        bright and believing in his stature
        and his grandeur in the world
He drives with his music loud
        and I can say a safe and joyous goodbye
        to the boy of deep devotion
        and run to greet the man
        of high hopes and soaring love

TEMPORARY TEARS

Sweet and bitter salty release
bathing the eye, lubricating, protecting
The overflow of life—
they cannot be contained but brim over
in a mysterious release and peace, from
        daily debris
        damaged emotions
        abuse and loss—onslaught of grief and pain

Tears fill the eyes without flowing
        from an awakened heart ambushed by love
        at the beauty of a sunset or a baby's dimpled skin
        or while embracing the prodigal ... home again

Let the lachrymal fluid flow
let the glistening drops descend
lest, stifled, they stultify the soul
Fresh bottled in heaven is every dewy drop
currency of this sphere only
In our awaiting other world
they will stop, and be no more!

THE OPEN GRAVE

Waves are lapping on the smooth white sands
    he so often strolled
on a day in the budding, promising month of May
    the first green blush on the fields he ploughed so often
He loved the sound and smells of the living earth
    of the newly turned turf awaiting the seed
A small group of the people he loved
    huddle by the open grave on this May morning

We are bereft

The casket, the dirt waiting to receive the remains
    to cover him in the dark dirt of his island home
Then the larks—a pair of them soaring and swooping—
    trill over the open grave
We lift our heads to see the song
    of a pair of birds, a pair of lovers reunited!
The light of heaven fills our sorrowing souls
    My mother and father together again
    after thirty long earthly years

THE GRACE

a hundred heads bowing
a nun invoking the blessing
for the simple spread
in a small crowded room
full of goodness and gratitude
humble and hopeful asylum seekers
bravely enduring the journey
of separation, the loss of so much
young heads bowed
eyes closed
letting the blessing bathe and still
their mesmerized minds
the reminder of Presence
beyond borders and boundaries
of largeness and love
Christo en mi
Christo en ti

EXCEPTIONAL EASTER

'Twas the morning of Easter
and throughout the earth
not a church bell was ringing
not an anthem heard singing
While confined to our quarters
we huddled together
in our ones and our twos

Just what to do
to celebrate him
our conquering King
who can't be confined to cloisters
but desires to be among the boisterous
to live as one with his wonderful people
having no need for stained glass or steeple

The risen Christ now in hearts resides
There he is now and forever abides

A CROWN OF FEAR

A microscopic virus
that is shaped like a crown
has made its home among us
for it cannot live without us
So, uninvited and unseen
we become unwitting hosts
to a most unwelcome guest
held hostage to its power
its potential and its scope!
A harbinger of doom
hacking at our reserves of hope
perturbing our peace and poise
The noise of fear thunders in
on every media outlet
anointing us with its merciless monarchy
We feel lost, helpless, dreading isolation

But peace will reign again
when we rein in the terror
and contemplate the error of forgetting
that this too shall pass
As together we coalesce inside
a much greater unseen Force
the Matrix of Love that holds all
our common, great Source
of Safety and Solace

II. RUMINATIONS
and REFLECTIONS

PERSPECTIVE

A baby burps and we croon
A tempestuous teen breaks wind and we gasp
in disapproving horror
We swoon over our infant's chubby hands
edible thighs and ticklish round belly
A pouting teenager daughter
is rebuked for eating too much and
sporting thunder thighs
A baby's toothless grin is heart melting
A grandpa's toothless grin is grimly grotesque

Ergo the power of perspective!

TILL THE END OF THE DAY

"Your child is disabled"
They assured me it was a gift
I am not sure they really knew
what else to say
It was for me to determine in what way
that could ever be

Now thirty tumultuous years later
we've travailed together,
the gift and the given,
the product of deep caring, despairing
and sharing the load. That little boy
can now hold a fishing rod, a job
the hand and heart of a girlfriend

The culmination of long, aching
days fraught with pain
from when he could not even
hold a pencil or a thought
Life with my beautiful, broken boy
remains hard. Though marred, we are
confident we will each be sustained
till the end of the day....

The gift part still eludes me
My life hovers on hold
I hold onto my God
He holds on to us both
The assurance of that grip,
well, that may be the gift

THE LOSS OF THE LAMBS

Oh! the meeting of the bleating
 of the mother ewes in mourning
 for the lambs torn from their bosoms
 to be fattened for the feeding of the man

Maternal anguish fills the pastures
 where the lambs were last seen leaping
 over hillocks young feet skipping
 with no glimpse of grieving yet to come

Daylight but dims in early summer here
 in northern climes where lamb is prime
 and the crying chorus fades not
 till the summer sun, in full, appears again

Then mollified mothers in quietude
chew the cud of forgetfulness

DAY OF DISSONANCE

I sat on the front porch swing
    maple syrup-sweetened mango tea
    a soothing elixir to the escalade of the day
Waves of shock and disappointment
    reverberated in rapid succession—
    a day of unexpected frustration

Adversarial and acrimonious service person
    I did not respond out loud
    eloquent, execution-style epithets unuttered
The man of the cloth who dismissed a dissident in class
    the hubris, the exclusion, stirred my despair
    shock and sorrow surged at the shaming
A friend on Facebook—could there be a safer space?
    bad day at the office
    snapping heads off on her way home!

My head and heart are quieted and calm
    I did not crumple under contrary circumstances
    Transcendence took the reigns

TIME PASSES

Slowly and painfully
while awaiting word of test results, or
for responses you long to hear from the estranged
while waiting for Santa or for the bell that
signals the end of silent meditation
　　(surely someone forgot to set the timer!)
time wends too slowly

Only too swiftly, though,
during summer days at the beach
skiing down winter wonderland slopes
scurrying to meet deadlines
savoring a lover's kiss
　　at the close of the final chapter
when they pass into timelessness

ONLY ONE WINNER

Two sides to every story
    that's what we see and hear
    in the courtroom where we sit
    in a jury of our peers

Reams of paper called exhibits
    shuffle, pile, proliferate
    with no certitude forthcoming
    though long, long the pontificate

WORD POWER

Words—endless deluge
torrents of shame and vituperation
pour out and pierce hearts
Someone is buried and bruised
under what we impart

Words flow ceaselessly
cascading, refreshing, reaching
deep into the center of the soul
Someone is revived and restored
in the rush of the water's flow

LOST AND FOUND

Leaving the love of a place
beginning to brace for the loss
  of the silence, the space, the serene
  what will it mean to be penned in
  hemmed around
  by endless sound in the city?

Feels like pity
closing in on my soul
  my cry
  my *why*
  have I ended up here
  robbed of my cheer!?

But there is more
I belong wherever I am
  There is more in store—
  lasting life hidden with God in Christ
  merely in another place
  living transcendently in glorious grace

PRAYING REWIND

The mighty flood of eloquent words
the marching army of accurate articulation—
and we think we have gotten through
to the source for a solution
to insurmountable issues that require revolution

Even if our scrupulous syntax
could suffice, could pay the price
to extract an answer from Above—
what about those whose tongues are tied
who know no words but those of tears?

Rewind to the start where Spirit abides
inside, no words required, only sounds
inarticulate groans that wrack the body—
this perfect prayer will bring resolution
to a mind so emptied of elocution

NO VERSE TODAY—

So what better to do than write about that
        about no words forming
        promising no performing
        in my head today?

Mind idling, assembling and essaying
        stilling in the storm of too much
        grief and angst and such
        roiling in the riot of present events

Like the sodden trees, their golden leaves
        drooping in the cold pre-snowfall rain
        what yesterday was glancing gold, perfectly plain
        my eloquence falls sodden to the ground

The darkness is illuminated in incremental light
        as the moon waxes and wanes in its cycles
        So for the poem: after seasons of stifles
        the full bright face of words will reappear

IN AWE OF ANGER

In its purest form only fifteen minutes long
Holding on and ruminating longer
becomes resentment, which we know is wrong

No longer the God-given, the fire of change
which kindles the flames that right the wrongs
Many whom we laud thought it not strange

or wallowed in guilt for being less than nice
when standing to be counted with the oppressed
to challenging the throwers of the dice

who lose their morals and their mind
imposing unjust statutes and laws
favoring the few, the less than, who are denied

a hearing, rights subtracted or burdens laid
on shattered shoulders, heavy hearts …
Let the fire be lit before it is said we were too afraid

to align with noble company. It is true
the apostle Paul advocated a knife
to castrate the newly converted but legalistic Jews

unlike the greatest of their kin who
wielded a whip in the desecrated temple
showing that to be angry is no sin

LOVE AND TRUTH ARE TWINS

What is Truth? asked Pilate
The accused, without hesitation, admitted he was
one identical to God
whose most majestic moniker is Love

We who walk in the Way of the Master
too often struggle with the twinning of the two
We are afraid that the truth will hurt,
that it is antithetical to love
Perhaps our love, devoid of truth, is not love at all
but a shallow pool that reflects our cowardice
our fawning fear of disturbing the status quo
of being rejected and disapproved

Take a gallop through the gospels
see the God-man at work!
Never flinching to speak boldly
against hypocrisy or ignorance or ignominy
eliciting truth from others
then laying down his life in unqualified love and devotion
for the ones he had chastised in their ignorance and pride

The deepest and dearest of lovers
count their own life dispensable
willing to lay personal comfort
reputation and acclaim
on the altar of suffering love
knowing that only truth can set us free

EMERGENT EPIPHANY

A rare stretch of straight English country road
a day of equally seldom seen sunshine
top down on my convertible
hair blowing
tears flowing

in a crisis of long forgotten fountainhead
a cry from the soul of a fearless, fanatical bible teacher
with color-coded scriptures for every creature
and every catastrophe
"I don't want to know any more *about* you,
I want to know you!"

Not from the open canopy of cerulean blue
but from the depths of a place in my soul
I only vaguely knew
came the thundering truth, with not a cloud in the sky
the riposte to my discouragement and dissonance
"I will show you, but don't put me into your formulas."

The birth pangs of a living relationship, ever-evolving
God of grace beyond rubric and rhetoric
revelation beyond time and space
less certitude while knowing more, but less defined
more mystery, the habitual hankering of my heart
mind ready for rewire, heart already on fire

WEARING OLD

I wear my old with
bold
below the fold, the news is
bright
the light of years distilled from
fears
that came and went
sent
in the nature of things, that finally
brings
freedom from expectations and dread
said
to truncate largeness of life and hope
scope
now headlines all in bold

III. SENSING SURROUNDINGS

IT'S RAINING

The rains that impede
      that feed
      the ground
We need its fruit
      the refreshing
Yet we feel trapped inside
      denied
      sapped of our energy
It's only wet
      why
      fret
Skip outside, greet
      the gentle kiss
      the refreshing bliss

ALTERNATIVE AMBIENCE

An empty lake
water wanting
no rain
no snow pack
only black mud
and grudging green
where grass alone is seen
where wide, deep water
used to fill the basin
now on its pockets of liquid
only a few birds glide
to reflect
the shallow
and the calm

RIVER REVERIE

how low the flow of the river
    now awaiting the spate of spring
soon to be folded in stratum
of serene snow and strong ice
    till a slice of warm sun
starts the cycle again

THUNDER

The rumbles get closer
Late afternoon in the mountains
Clouds stacked and black
Showtime in the playground of the sky ...
The air heavy with promise of rain!

Then delicious drops descend
Anticipation of torrents to follow
Opening the dry hot thirsty earth
Whose gratitude is ascending scents
Broken vials releasing sweet perfume

MONOCHROMATIC MUSINGS

I selected the swatches
  so the match was
  perfectly blended with the barks
  of the tall, tall ponderosa pines
  abutting my diminutive deck
  freshly painted to be one with the trees
  plastic rocker from Lowes, same color!
I convene with these
  sip coffee in morning light
  and as night knits the darkness
  I sip fine evening wine
Wind soughs through the branches
  filigree fingers of needles
  dance under darkening skies
Then from the top to the roots' toes
titan trunks shiver and sway at wind's whim
  no resistance
  no insistence
  no distance
  from the invisible force that dictates the
  Source of the Dance
A marked muse mellows my mind
  my cocoon invaded
  my sacred space expanded
In my Secret Garden I am reminded
  not to harden my heart
  to the winds that blow
They are part of the whole
  scattering my seeds to the ground

DIAMOND DANCE

Diamonds of sun dance on the water ...
the water buoying the birds
the birds that nest and sing
the singing that heralds spring
spring up all around
Diamonds dance on me ...

BIRDS COMING BACK

In the dawning it dawned on me
there was a silence that should not be
    no birdsong, no flight, no sight of droppings
    no fallen feathers on the ground
    not a birdsong, not a sound

Where had the birds gone? How long
had I not noticed the absence of song
    of twitter and bustle in the branches
    from cardinals to mockingbirds to doves!
    our family of flight out of reach of our love

Empty skies, as plane-less as the day after nine eleven,
drinking my coffee alone at seven
    a sense of abandonment, almost apocalyptic!—
    given we're all of one Lover's intention, one unified field
    a togetherness to which I gladly yield

Full feeders, the fountain beckoning for a bath
no predators, no known fears along this path
    Perished, poisoned by neighbors, unaware?
    Or they may have enough fresh grass seed
    from nearby new-house lawns, all they need

As if to tell me this was so, the very next day
    a pair of lowly, lovely doves perched on a wire
    to feed my hope of an avian return:
"We will be back; times and seasons, there is a reason"
No fear, calm and assurance, expectation; not treason!

DUCKS ON THE WATER

They glide as on ice
This looks effortless
They part the still lake waters
and leave large silky swathes in their wake
on a surface of velvet, in perfect Vs
If we could see under the surface …
Why! there are two webbed feet
fiercely peddling; propellers, the power
underneath and unseen
Outwardly it often seems
I am operating in tandem with a Spirit
who is steering, gliding as gracefully as the duck does
No one would ever guess that beneath my calm exterior
many times there are mighty machinations (such as the)
   agitation that propels me
   anxiety that fuels me
   alone and self-severed from my Source....

The unruffled exterior deceives
only those standing on the shore

SPRING WITHOUT A STEP

I've never heard the birds so loud
   the rose bush so bursting full of blooms
Have the fruit trees always bowed
   beneath yields of sweetness to be consumed?
This spring the world stood still
   suspended in twilight 'twixt bright and night
Nature rallied and surged, to assure
   their halting human family they'd be all right

REMEMBERING THE RIDE

I well recall …
the smell of the saddle,
the surge of the strength
the scarcely restrained power
the palpable excitement
muscles quivering in anticipation
unleashing the power
the pride of the ride
the becoming one
the morphing of rider and horse
        the walk
        the trot
        the canter
        the gallop
the thrill of the will
of two in tandem
terrifying, thrilling and free
thundering through the trees
under cerulean Colorado skies

Memories made with a friend
long absent from tethered earth
I fully expect her
to ride her five-gait steed
in that celestial sphere!

HYACINTH IN THE LABYRINTH

I bought a pot of hyacinths in bloom today …
I do that every year at this time
for they were my father's favorite flower
They say memories grow dimmer as days pass
but my recollection of him, his presence and aura
are as vivid as the strong scent
as wondrous as the raceme of flowers on each stem
I selected blue ones; he seemed to like that color best
Though so long laid to rest, he soars the skies
in a labyrinth of possibilities, of never-ending beauty
and I am sure the hyacinth is hiding there,
its distinct perfume giving it away

Say not memories grow dimmer by the day …

AN ANGLE OF REPOSE

The steep angle of descent …
more weight of this earth
and we will slump
like a pile of dirt heaped too high
dumped, to reach the sky!
Interlocked with others—
not separate grains, but larger rocks
can buffer the shocks,
sustain the slant,
and point to the sky
As children scamper up and down,
the slopes of dirt facilitating
their play, may we be ready ramps
of hope for those who need to recreate
on the Rock of our rest and repose

IV. TAKES ON THEOLOGY

PLENTY FOR ALL

Jesus rallied the multitude under the banner of Plenty
    ever alert to endless evidence of humanity's hunger
On hillsides teaming with thousands he made
    a plenteous picnic from fragmented fish and broken bread
In effect he said, there is always enough
    in the foison of the Father's world
On a beach where they launched abandoned fishing boats
    they floated off shore without a catch
Those nail-scarred hands served disciples who had fled,
    who had betrayed and deserted him
The aroma of God's homemade breakfast
    beckoned and sated their stricken souls

They knew him by the breaking of the bread
    he who took less and made it more
    who calls us to raise the flag of the Kingdom come
    that points to the place of more than enough
    our source, supply, and sufficiency; no scarcity
Our privilege: to welcome, find, and feed both friend and foe

THE PARACLETE

Teacher
of all truth, unspoken
of things left untaught by Jesus
to elucidate what is already written

Intercessor
who prays perfectly
with unutterable inner groans
when we know not how to pray

Emissary
from the Father
as a descending dove
announced the Lamb of God

Comforter
never left the Son of Man
in the wilderness facing the foe
nor in the crucible of history, the cross

Advocate
birthed the church in fire
took up residence in and among us
sealed our place in the filial family divine
secured our place in the circle of eternal Love

PRESENCE IN THE PRESENT

He is
the I AM
always present tense
folding in love so immense
clinging to hope
when certainty elopes

He is
the I Am
ever pleading our case
all accusation erased
nothing to fear
we are loved, in the clear

He is
the I Am
closer than breath
for our journey on earth
the air beneath our wings
when we fly free from earthly strings

LOVE THAT WILL NOT ...

We, and every bird that sings
every blade that brings forth fruit
every worm that burrows in the ground
connected, founded in the desire

of Universal Intelligence
called the Christ
he who loved all into sentience
and proclaimed it sacred and good

tuning the benevolent beating of our hearts
setting the rhythm of every breath
synchronizing every life force to start
and stay, to adapt in awesome array

All creation retains the imprimatur of Love
of a sapience greater than our limitations
Who conducts the orchestra of miraculous grace
in wild beauty of wilderness and restless seas

May we become aware, and face-to-face
with one another, animal, mountain and meadow
behold the wonder of our world hung in space
the value and worth of the broken and bent

And with reverent, tender compassion
love all with the same passion that sent the first cell
into life-pulsing perpetuity; the offspring of divinity,
of love that will not let go

THE ULTIMATE CRY

On the Roman torture of a common cross
hung he who claimed to be one with God
Lashed by a whip studded with metal and bone bits
Scalp lacerated by the crown of twisted thorns
His wrists nailed to the wooden gibbet
The excruciating, pulsing pain
blinded his mind and soul
He was immobilized and bloodied

How was it possible that his God got up and left
that he abandoned his very own child?
The God he told us about, the one
who loves relentlessly, forgives, never forsakes
So when he cried, and they heard
"My God, my God, why have you forsaken me?"
a familiar psalm that some bystanders might recall
and be persuaded of yet another fulfillment of prophecy—
that he was indeed the Christ!

How did theologians far removed from that
day of cosmic chaos
ever get the narrative so wrong …
that God was too holy to look upon the sin bearer?
Tearing the Trinity asunder is a fateful blunder
If they be true then Jesus lied, blasphemed,
was not in union with his Father when
he healed the sick and forgave sins, dined with sinners
wept with them, ate with them, died for them …

No, this cry from the depths of the unthinkable
from his human heart, identifying with us,
his earthly family
the stalking sense of utter abandonment from our Source
Where are you God?
The outpouring anguish of the ages
This was the cry of our beautiful big brother to his Father,
at one with us,
feeling our fear that God was not near
The One who could never disappear—
Jesus, the Christ, was still one with God

WHERE IS GOD?

In a world writhing in pain
we ache for a cogent theodicy
Where is God in the midst?
If he is so omnipotent
    why is he so impotent
If he is omniscient
    surely he could divert the disasters
If he is omnipresent
    how can he bear to witness
    perpetual anguish
    of his aching world?

Easy answers are elusive ... but

In the endless need
    he is everywhere
I last saw him
    in the form of a brave bilingual man
    picking up dead bodies
    left behind in the desert
    where they dropped in their weakness
    on the road to freedom

DEADLY DENIAL

Refusal to look at the locked-up past
the wounds that still bleed
seep, drain our life blood
into an abyss of loss—
canyons of darkness

Come to the light
naked. In plain sight
of the Healer
whose shameless salve
stems the flow

Light beams in
seals the wound
till only the scar remains
only showing where
the chains had bound

Badges of beauty
despite blame and pain
all turned to gain
Now the wounded one is a healer too—
that is me, that is you

JESUS IS

I hear many say
Jesus is great
I find no fault in him
He is cited by those who have a cause
who want to show he cares
whereas the church is full of flaws
You are right, not being trite
I agree, we have represented him poorly
We have been hypocrites and worse
But you have been selective
in your flirtatious association
with he who claims
to be God in the flesh

Jesus is not the mascot of anyone's cause
Applause he does not need or demand
He belongs not to religion or race—
But the lover we long for
the comforter we ache for
who blames no one
prefers no one
no one excluded—
He belongs to all
We all belong to him

THE COSMIC CHRIST

The Christ who came at Christmas
has always been
though not seen
until he came as Jesus
    God with us
Religion can cripple The Christ
make weak and mild
he who is the wild
who created the Cosmos
    God has come to us
the Source of all that is and was
beginning and the end
he who would blend
Heaven and earth
    The God-man is here
The Christ who is the Voice
He is the one who speaks
He is the one who seeks
not power but union
    God and man as one
So Love came down at Christmas
and wrapped us naked newborns,
aching to be held. Behold the meld,
the Divine entrusted in a body
    God is not God without us

SCARS THAT REMAIN

The slash on his side
the hammered hands
the wounds Thomas touched
convinced the doubter
this is the Jesus
he knew. Yet we
who never knew Jesus
of Nazareth, now know
with equal conviction
the ascended Christ
the Son of Man
one of our kind
now sits in the heavens
with Father and Spirit,
all of us embedded
in seamless union
with the eternal Triune
The scars are evidence
The scars remain

THE LORD'S PRAYER

Oh, Our Father!
who has now come to indwell
the fleshly tabernacle of our souls ...
Why do we still address you as far away!
Has not your Kingdom come to stay, in us?—
our mandate to turn the world upside down
by Spirit who works in us to do your will on earth

Do we not partake daily of the living bread of life
feasting by faith on the Body of him
broken for our sake
sated and wanting nothing we already have
We have surely been fully and forever forgiven
Every accusation against us was driven
into those healing hands

The New Covenant sealed with his blood
empowers us to resist evil, renders us out of its reach
as Grace has overtaken law and its condemnation
The unutterable name of YAHWEH
now lilts from our lips in highest praise
as simple as breathing in and out: Our Father! who art
on earth in us, as we are, in the heavens, with you—

Holy, Holy is your Name

FORGIVE

As you have been forgiven
    is what we are told
be bold, render the same to others:
But do I know the depth of my abhorrence
the torrents of shame and guilt
that swirl in my deepest unconscious?—
Tell me if I have forgiveness for those?

Even in repose I project my proclivities on others
    is what I am told
What needs forgiving? …
every frivolous infraction?
only the major malfeasance
where good has been murdered
in the power of my weakness?
wielded in wrath and fear and pain
again and again

Have I been forgiven?
Must I make a list?
It will be long
and have blanks,
times when I did not know what I was doing

Wait! for they know not what they do
If they had known they would not have
crucified the Christ
Forgiven simply because we are innocent and ignorant
adrift at the mercy of Love!
No list of naughty or nice …

As ice melts in the warmth of the sun
every offense evanesced, erased from the record
    so we are told
Not even the faintest recollection
of a debit column

If I had known better
I would not have done the wrong
Neither would you
Humanity sings a new song
since that mocking crowd of criminals
were fully forgiven—
    So I believe

THE VIRGIN MARY

At Advent I love to ponder this teenaged girl, Mary
    "one who endured much pain and suffering"
Many had that name in an occupied land of fear and
    dread, where young girls became soldier's playthings
This Mary became God's favored pick
    to be the womb of his incarnation
I am in awe and wonder at her obedience, song,
    rejoicing young heart, paramount trust in YAHWEH

She, becoming the mother of my God in the flesh
    cried and rocked with pain as he came
She held him fiercely, then fled to another land—
    refugees at God's bidding
Later, she took him to the Temple
    and lost him, and worried
Using her mama ways she persuaded him
    to turn water into wine at that wedding

And now, my Catholic family of faith believes
    she can intercede on their behalf too
This daughter of the Reformation ponders the story
    and wonders, why not? With my sister Mary
I believe "with God all things are possible"
    I, the evidence of one man's prayer to Mary, became
the best wine, his bride, saved as the last gift of time
    At Advent I ponder this woman …

THE GREAT EXCHANGE

Would you rather be a penitent
    standing alone
    before a throne
    of a merciless judge
    who carries a grudge
than know the Arbiter who
    finds us faultless
    has dismissed the charges
    destroyed the files
    in the fire of his trials?

The Argus of the law has no face
Now we breathe and bask only in grace

V. VOICES OF WOMEN

ANTHEM FOR ANNA

So, was your anthem loud, raspy but robust
as you burst out loud and full of song
while Simeon was praying?
Your exuberance knew no bounds
Was the infant in the Temple with his parents
the promised Deliverer, come to ransom lonely exiles?
I am sure you watched and listened from a distance
strained to hear and see with very old eyes and ears
I am sure you longed to hold that precious child
you who never snuggled or smelled a baby of your own
You spread the news to all who came to the Temple
accosting all who hoped, who like you, longed
for the freedom of the Holy City
So long a widow, missing and longing
giving yourself to the singular service of your God
trusting his faithfulness to you and the House of Israel

Fasting and praying night and day,
for what did you so endlessly implore?
Did you hear that we, Gentiles of whom you knew nothing,
were also included in the prophecy of Simeon?
As he held the God-man, the baby from Bethlehem
did you know you were interceding for all of us, too?
So many questions for the almost unknown Anna
far away and ancient Jewish sister
You now are in the Presence of what you looked forward to
I am there, too, by faith in what I look back upon
We now, together, sing praises of him upon the Throne

WOMEN

I salute you
    bone of my bone
    from that first rib
I exult in the brave ones
    ache with the hurt ones
    celebrate the successful
    who remain kind
I refuse to be anyone's political pawn
    degraded
    downgraded
    by any religion
We are enough—
    equal, yes
    but more mutual—
    That's how this world will work
As we take our noble place alongside,
    eschewing even a hint
    of victimhood
    We are good—
Someone who matters said so

MY JEWISH FRIEND

We worked together
   She was warm, witty, bright
When I thought I had the God-thing right
   back in my narrow-thinking days

Though forbearing of my zeal,
   she made it very clear
that no matter what the deal
   no one was privy to all His ways

She felt not love and caring
   in my abundant sharing
but rather a notch awaiting a place on my belt
   I'll never forget that and how I felt

It would surprise her to know what she left behind
   besides her warmth and wisdom …
She always put her panties on over her tights
   I now see that, too, as so very right!

SEQUINS BEFORE SIX

Noon at Starbucks
midst sweat suit set and
hikers with rucksacks
there she sits
ruby red lips
scarlet sequined dress

From a see-through baggie
she pulls out pills
some for him, sitting still
some for her, red nails glistening
no longer listening
for the call to hike hills
or be enslaved to workouts

Devotion in slow motion
the two of them
coffee and cakes
and water for the pills

MY SONG OF SONGS

Your infinite care of me
   so tender
   so patient
   so intimate
can scarcely be shared
When I feel less than worthy, you wrap me
in a blanket of adoring approval

Your presence is so personal
   faithful friend
   I, faithless
   frightened
You know what will bring back the smile
on my crumpled countenance
when I fear you frown from afar

They manifest as miracles to me, my Lord
   a letter
   a phone call
   a bird song
Like a long lost treasure reappearing
delivered in the nick of time
by you who know my every whim

You come and dance me through the night
   with balloons
   and bunting
   and the music of the stars
You have seduced me with your goodness and grace
My eyes turn to the skies and see
the banner over me is Love

I feel your touch as that of a Lover's
    catching my teardrops
    in the wounded Hands
    of caring caresses
Now we are one, Christ in me and I in him
The long nights of fleeting visits are over …
Morning has come, O! Shulamite* sister!

*the woman featured in Song of Solomon

DULL EARS, LOUD THOUGHTS

What? Please stop mumbling, will you all?
I want so much to respond to the call
of whatever you say or see
Just stop and think of the aging of me—

Whose ears have heard a thousand bird songs
weathered painful political speeches way too long
the first to hear your cry as you entered the earth,
to rejoice in your good news, weep in your dearth

Whose ears have heard pronouncements so dire
outbreaks of war, a world forever, somewhere, on fire
A woman who bore the pain of hearing she is less than
Scalded with wounding words from too many men

Whose ears of the heart have stores of sagacity to share
Who so longs to divulge the diversions through despair
to those who would listen and hear
to those who would come close, come near

So come closer beloveds, face to face
Lean in till I can feel your breath, a long journey retrace
Tell me your story too, I so want to know
what you think and feel, curiosity I will never outgrow

HOMAGE TO HARPER

Colorful canes
bright mind
my feisty friend Harper
none sharper
Fiercely opposed to fools
filled with pools of compassion for the broken
brooking no bargain with those who exclude any
especially the rights of women among the many

Tender with the broken wings
of all animals and sentient things
the same with the old and lame
Courage without measure
in the treasure of her one precious person
whose heart and mind were large and loud
Only her body betrayed her and became undone

No "rest in peace" for Harper
Fly free, my wonderful friend
You have left that wheelchair behind you

You have also left a hole in my heart
that only you could fill

VI. THE DARKER SIDE

THE DEPRESSING

pressing
am being crushed
distressing
disintegrating
darkness thickens
whatever mission the minion is on
it has won for now
I am crashing and all is blackness

the grip will loosen, the light will shine
and entwine my spine in strength again
now buckling under condemnation
a proclamation of deliverance
that always anchors the darkness
seeps through my veins
my mind
my body
and soul
back in control
the troll of darkness vanishes into the air
like a wisp of smoke whose fire has gone out

DISCARDED

all the parts must be counted
       two arms
       two legs
On the table they are mounted
       the crushed brain
       contents drained
Out of the safety of the womb
       this child
       will never bloom
The tiny arms will never reach out
       to the sound of the speech
       of his mother
The chubby legs will never run
       to be spun in the air
       by her father
And what of the mind
       housed in
       that brain?
The world looks in vain
       for the gift
       it contained

BETRAYAL

Where were you
    when the false accusations flew
Did you only care
    when the days were fair?
Were you too ashamed of my stance—
    too self protective perchance?
So you left me standing alone
    bewildered and broken
to atone for my truth, my convictions
    that cut across the traditions
I will miss you on the journey, friend
    But I will listen for your footsteps round the bend

THE WIDOW

Becoming a widow
is no small thing
not just the removing of the ring
that has bound
you, that found
you, so long ago

It is surgery sans anesthesia
savage segmentation
cut loose as if in space
weightless and wandering
the familiarity of the earth once known
now hollow, hostile foreign soil

Will a morning ever dawn
that sorrow won't live on
in the rising of the sun?
Tears dry but should flow forever
given the severity of the severance
and the gaping grief of the grave

OBSERVED AT THE CAR DEALER

Shaking in his aged weakness, he enters the doors
    then shuffles in over the marble floor
He is surely not considering buying a car?
    Maybe he drives round the block … not far!
He frowns feebly under the burden of lost youth
    Has he faced the truth?:
Just how would it feel—
    a sleek, gleaming casket of Lexus steel?

Though I know not the full story
    it appears gone are days of glory
The power of the horses under the hood
    a mere memory roaring loudly down the road
Now dimly dawdling away …
    Not today; not buying today

FINAL ANALYSIS

If I should fail or fall
   if sheer weariness wins the race
   before I break the ribbon,
   remember me for what I did before I tripped

To finish well is the grandest goal, lest we become
   unknown and unsung
   relegated to the echo chamber of the song
   we once sang so strong

Our deluge of dicta languishing
   in lonely piles and over-full files
   forgotten. That which we so fiercely defended,
   were so sure of, now unread, irrelevant

So quickly one false step sullies a lifetime of labor
   Mercy is in short supply
   to those once loudly lauded,
   who loved so long and worked so hard

An icy aura of abandon envelops the memory
   like relentless waves
   erasing footsteps in the sand
   as the tide approaches

Now to him Who is able
to keep us from falling …

DISTRAUGHT

A string that is taut
awaiting just one more thought of
> Dismay
> Disappointment
> Disrespect

And there is no more tune to play
For all that anyone can say
is dissonant and far away
happy and glad submerged in sad
The Dance goes on and I am dragged behind
hoping to find my muse
to use the inward compass
to magnetic north
the irresistible draw of the filings of my soul
to gather in the
> Density
> Divine
> Dear

And hear the Voice again
with no echoes of shame,
the same entreaty to be
me, the one and only
> Embraced
> Endlessly
> Emphatically approved

THE LEDGE OF LONELINESS

A chasm of fear yawns; will she be forgotten while she lives
      the phone stay silent
      the email box bereft of correspondence
      no message tone to herald a welcome connection?
Tiptoeing on the ledge of loneliness

As life's pace slows down, fewer schedules to keep
      no one clamoring for her advice
      her experience now deemed dated
      the shelf life of her input impotent, expired
Fingers fumbling the ledge of loneliness

I held her till she saw the rosebud
      felt the gentle breeze
      heard the mockingbird sing
      the peace a prayer can bring
Till she slipped back and away from the ledge

DISTILLING THE DYSTOPIA

Thick and tainted, it starts as a trickle. Now the air we
breathe has to be filtered by inept masks. The invisible
enemy permeates everything, we are told.

> *No air is there for one man pinned to the ground,*
> *for soon there is no sound.*

While the sounds of labored breathing wreak lungs across
the globe, fear blankets the earth. We have to stay home,
isolated from all familiar, from all essential to good health,
the gift of touch from others.

> *One man is held in a firm grip, an unwelcome touch*
> *that finally takes his breath away!*

The air we breathe grows thicker still.

> *Now choking on a rage so deep, an infection so long*
> *incubating in the inner reaches of the soul, thousands*
> *teem onto the city squares, breathing terror and hate and*
> *fear. Statues—of those considered complicit—crumble,*
> *for they are deemed an affront to the memory of*
> *unbreathing ones.*

Morgues pile high with bodies, breathing stopped
because of a very present enemy. They are dying alone.
Burials delayed for fear of meeting the same fate.
When will all be whole? When will we gather in carefree
laughter, spilling over one another in riotous joy?—
After the distances are discarded!
Fear is the common cause, the source of the dying
for want of breathing the pure air of love, free to all!
LOVE comes carrying solutions to heal the present
that paralyzes, and solvents to disperse the past that
imprisons.

DARK BLOOD

How did the earth
ever absorb the blood
of the slaughtered millions?
How did the open graves
ever close over
the heaps of bones
from the gas chambers?
Did anyone ever hear the groans from the humus?

Heaps of humanity discarded into the darkness of
the womb from which they came
The good earth co-opted into carrying out the crime
of annihilation
becoming a tomb
human particles penetrating the dirt
feeding the soil
where the grass will grow

Feeding the soil
where flowers will be planted
where a coffee shop will sprout
sporting a plaque of remembrance
for six million Jews
whose essence is not found in the dirt of Dachau
but vibrates as imperishable waves in the Presence
of the God of Abraham, Isaac, and Jacob

Flesh and bone of our own
live on in indestructible glory

A GLOBE IN GRIEF

Staggering through the stages, all ages
Surely a mistake was made, manufactured, and
misinformation …
First surging shock, this surely cannot be!
Denial

We huddle in our houses, sealed and sanitized
Resentment and rage pulse through
the miasma of bewilderment
What is or is not true? We argue, banished into isolation
Anger

A closed system of despair
drowns the sound as the mad
makes way for the sad
The darkness helps to distance the pain
Depression

Let's see, surely we have sinned greatly
and grieved the capricious gods?
Prayer chains link round the globe pleading, promising …
Our fault. For what? No response …
Bargaining

We fix our gaze on the horizon of news and "experts"
But the sun never quite makes it to the zenith of light
No warmth. We shiver. Our nadir dips further in the sky
of hope for what … Might Be!
Acceptance

We are quieted; clarity of thought at low watermark
Dullness covers the earth as the tide goes out
Not sure of its return to shore as before!
Settling to be safe, but not free
No fight left?

THE BORDER DUST

While there are walls and gates
growing and groaning before them
heavy with hate and fear
they swell the sanctuaries, hurting and hoping
for openings to freedom
fleeing from oppression, hunger and killing
willing to work, build a home in the pursuit of happiness
looking into the eyes of his young wife
holding their tiny baby like a swaddled refugee of old
wrapping up against the cold of the winter desert
the desert of dirt and desolation, inhospitable, cruel
claiming lives, shedding blood

Have we failed to notice, in the shuffle of the documents
in the weary, dreary arguments, the for and against …
that the dust of the desert is no different
either side of the Wall
that the blood that collects among the cactus
runs as red as it does on fine linens
in beds across the Border

LACHRYMAL LAMENT

They spring
   not from self-pity
   not even from anger or fear
   which at the moment clings so near
   that settles like dust in the mind when
   at the first wind of words with dire projections
   blows throughout the body, invades
   every nook and cranny, settling in the cells
No, these tears seep slowly to the surface
   eyes weary of the sadness, the privation, the grief
   the accumulated sorrow, the loss, the robbery
   by the thief of peace and patterns and people and joy
We mourn. Gone is the fun, the freedom, the industry
the commerce, the concerts
   sports without spectators
   classrooms without students and teachers
   dreams on hold
   disappointment deep and rife
A virus-tipped sword
   lacerates liberty, eviscerates hope
   terminates lives in rasping, gasping breath
Alone! We are together, alone
   Isolation is not our milieu
   Distance is not our destiny
   May we touch again soon
   hold on long, and laugh
   and dance to the presently muted music
Let torrents of tears cascade in cathartic release

VII. THE LIGHTER SIDE

BLOOD LINES

When I was small
and would fall
I wondered as I saw
the red blood
     on the ground …
Did the princess shed
her blood of blue
when she slipped
and fell
     on the palace floor?

EXPLETIVES

Well, now! When we get to fussin' and frettin'
what are you bettin'
that a less than choice word
might not escape the pursed lips
of even the most righteous
    about to trip

A slip of the tongue, not intended
Surely such speech can be defended
in a time of abject anger, frustration, fear
No time to marshal a modulated moniker
the simple expletive so accessible
    so very near

No lightning bolt from heaven strikes
though many, including you, dislike
Let no shame or guilt demand you grovel
'Tis but a word with suitable sounds
that satisfies the situation
    But Grace abounds

Cussin' is common, easy and fast
not the language that lasts
not what adorns our highest prose
Aimed at people, not things, it hurts and wounds
So we aim to select sweet syllables that bless
    erasing expletives before they balloon

BUSINESS CALL

In the middle of the muse
   as words were in spate
   poetry in the peak of production
   the river of creative juices running wild
my gentle, genius broker broke in with news,
   all good, of my account

To *How are you?*
   came a mirage of metaphor sublime
   about sucking the marrow out of life
   and learning to field the rogue balls

A short silence
   that transmitted the sound of a smile

Then, to *How is your family?*
   yet another soaring song lauding
   good seasons and all the reasons
   my vibes were so high

A gentle goodbye from a man of matchless manners
   who tried to match my heady pitch and tone
   not allowing the slightest lacuna to lever his thoughts
Then he was gone to share with his colleagues
   the too much information conversation, and
   what happened to *Just fine* and *Thank you!*?

WORDS THAT WORKED

My sagacious mother loved the Book
She quoted freely to her family and brooked
no disregard for the Holy Word
So I listened and knew and never unheard …

"A word to the wise is sufficient," which implied
if you are smart, no need to repeat or further chide
Such clever bribery to obey!
Of course I will choose the right and say

only the good and the true, don't fret
"For thou, God, doth see me!" How can I forget?
My mama's appeals to a higher calling
embedded in me fear of failing and falling

and kept me awake at night
as I recalled the scripture that seemed so right
"Never let the sun go down on your wrath," she said
Till the matter was resolved, no sleep had I upon my bed

ON BEING A VEGETARIAN—

on Thanksgiving Day
oneness
family
camaraderie
gratitude
grief for the millions of slaughtered turkeys
on this celebratory day of the year
smiles
loves
laughter
lightness
heaviness for the living creatures, dead and carved,
quibbled over; there is a correct cutting procedure
patience
gentleness
tenderness
thankful
acceptance of others' comfortable convictions,
of my otherness; absence of adjudication
united
included
heard
honored
HAPPY!

CHANGES

Somehow those emails that herald new Internet protocol
        regarding my billing and various vendors—
Changes are coming that will—
        make it easier, not

My heart quakes, all exultant expectations eclipsed
        by the prospect of creating a new password
Do you have any idea how many of those I have already?
        No. I don't even know

Yet another is not happy news, because I forget them
        —don't file them well
Could we please just
        leave well alone!

A PRAYER FOR THE FESTIVE SEASON

Lord, may I remember....
    You love all the celebrations, not because
      we give thanks or bless the baby Jesus
      But because you love your
      crazy, wierd, wonderful
       messed-up and hurting humanity
       with whom you are so melded
    When we cry, you cry
      When we laugh, you laugh
      When we love, it is your love

May I remember, Father …
    You are with me as I shop for the food and gifts
    You understand needs and wants
      without censorious assessment of which is which
    You love the smile of the child at what Santa brought
      and the cook's delight when the pie looks perfect
    You hug Uncle Harold a bit more when he is grumpy
      and mother-in-law when she is full of critique
    The friend who always gets tipsy?—
      You hold her steady on the way home

May I remember, precious Lord …
    You love a party bursting with song and dance
    Life is a romance as we raise our glasses
      for the good things,
      toasting trees and turkeys
      candles and wreaths
      babies and ancients

No thing and no one is sent without your imprint
    without your blessing
    your approval and your love

May I remember, glorious God …
    You cannot but be present
        no matter how ersatz our extravagances
    The pleasure of your company is assured
        though uninvited, unheralded, unseen
May I remember, dearest Lord Christ …
    Your Presence is procured by decree
    Where we are, you are, and always will be
May I remember, is my prayer!

SOME OF MY FAVORITE THINGS

Blood orange infused olive oil
   from Temecula Valley
Smooth newly washed white sheets
   blown dry in a dancing wind
The smell of a new book
   (I bury my face in the pages)
A cackling log fire in my cabin
   warning winter we are hidden and held
A new pen that writes smooth and round
   (I delight in the words it forms)
A pine-scented candle flickering
   in the care of the kitchen
A polished tabletop
   with woods gleaming smooth and strong
A piano concerto by Chopin
   untethering my soul
The first sliver of the sun through the trees
   lighting up the runway of my day
The fading light heralding the night
   marshaling my musings as slumber strolls in

LITTLE THINGS

a sticky note in the lunch bag
    words of affirmation and love
flowers for no reason
    no season required
a crumpled letter carried
    in a purse for years
    sent in caring at a time of grief
giving away a favorite item
    because someone admires it so
two poinsettias for a dollar from my son
    delivered in the dark rain of the morning
remarking on the green eyes of the rescue puppy
    who barked loudly at a crowded party
    diverting distress for the hostess

Little things lighten the load

ACKNOWLEDGEMENTS

Grateful thanks to my daughter, Sandra, whose eagle eye read and edited the manuscript; to my son, Grant, for his formatting pictures to prose; and to my Arizona-based grand boys, whose technical abilities and adroit accessing of the internet are indispensable to me, a generation removed from its mystery!

To all who encourage me to write poetry by your affirming of my work, I thank you. For a wondrous world of beauty and goodness, I am in perpetual praise! I am equally indebted to the pain and the pathos, the fears and the doubts, those of my own and of others, that enlarge my soul in lament and contemplation. Most of all, I am grateful for a God of grace who holds both the "good" and the "bad" in the matrix of Love.

I am blessed beyond measure, for having a faithful and trusted editor whose integrity, grace and honesty is the stuff of pure joy with which to work. Thank you Cathy!

And finally, a shout-out to my newfound friend and astonishing artist, Elaine Pedersen. Her work is the color signature of the words you find assembled in this volume of poetry. Her art is what draws the eye to the cover and that entices exploration of what is inside *Unpaused.* I am honored to have found you and that you grace this work with your art, Elaine!

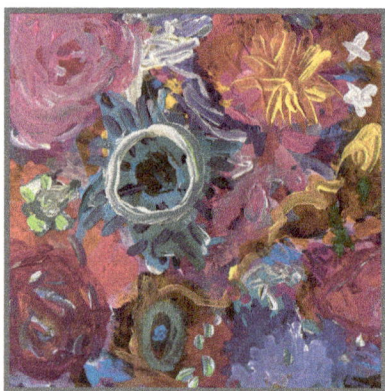

ABOUT THE POET

Alice Scott-Ferguson is a Scottish-born freelance writer and motivational speaker. She was educated as a registered nurse in Scotland, holds a B.S. in Health Sciences, and has worked mainly in the psychiatric field.

She has contributed to both the secular and religious press, has authored several Bible studies and written prize-winning poetry. Her first book *Little Women, Big God* was published in 1999 and is the story of the women's ministry she founded and directed in the U.K.

An engaging and enthusiastic speaker, Alice has traveled internationally, presenting at various venues—women's seminars, writers workshops, and conferences for both women and men. She is passionately committed to bring God's liberating love and freedom to her audience. She continues to lead Bible study classes each week locally, and her passion is ever to teach and live out the fierce, limitless love of God.

Her book *Mothers Can't Be Everywhere, But God Is* was first released by Cladach Publishing in 2002 and re-released in 2018.

Alice co-authored, with Nancy Parker Brummett, *Reconcilable Differences: Two Friends Debate God's Role for Women* (2006, David C. Cook)

A collection of Alice's poetry, *Pausing in the Passing Places*, was released in 2018 by Cladach Publishing.

Alice was widowed several years ago and has since remarried. Her family has now extended to include four step children and ten step grandchildren in addition to her own three natural children and six grandchildren who are scattered across the country.

Alice and her husband live in Phoenix, Arizona.

www.ingramcontent.com/pod-product-compliance
Lightning Source LLC
Chambersburg PA
CBHW050824090426
42738CB00021B/3476